Run to Boston

Poems for the Marathoner

By

Julie B Hughes

First published by Julie B Hughes 2021

Run to Boston

Copyright © 2021 by Julie B Hughes

Julie B Hughes asserts the moral right to be identified as the author of this work.

Photo credit About Author page :

Alice G Patterson @alice@agpphoto.com

First edition

ISBN: 978-1-7376907-3-3

This book was professionally typeset on Reedsy.
*Find out more at **reedsy.com***

To marathoners,

Keep chasing your dream and never give up! The love of running is a gift and what connects us.

Onward and Upward!

Contents

Running Joyful and Free

Running joyful and free
Was the Lord's gift to me
He had a plan all along
The country roads are where I grew strong

Yet pain took over as the years flew by
The power I no longer had
The tears filled my eyes

What is wrong with me?
Why is this happening?
These questions occupied my mind
It wasn't helpful
And left me more in a bind.

I had a dream that kept me going
I wasn't going to give up
Not without knowing
What does this pain mean?
What can I do?

These questions turned me down the right path

Of the lessons, I needed to learn
The new knowledge brought me back
To understand my pain and keep me on track

I'm running again, joyful and free
My dream came true!
Thank you, Lord, for being you

———◆———

Dream

The dream began in 1998
To run the Boston Marathon
It was going to be great!
I was eager to run in 2003
Yet my body and mind didn't agree

The pain took over
It consumed my days
I wanted to keep running
Yet I couldn't find a way

The shame was rooted deep
Yet God had a plan
He gave me the strength to look inward
Face my fears and not hide
He never left my side

To follow my dream
I would need to let go
The burdens I was still carrying
Too many, I know

I held tight to courage
And began to unpack
My load getting lighter
As my runs were coming back

I will not give up on my dream
I am brave, strong, and free
I choose love
And connection is key

———◆———

Take a Chance

Take a chance
lace up your sneakers
Take a chance
step out the door
Take a chance
run a block and back
Take a chance
run 2 or 3 blocks more

Take a chance
run 2 or 3 times a week
Take a chance
run 3 or 4 times more
Take a chance
your building a practice
Take a chance
running consistently is now the norm

Take a chance
sign up for a race
Take a chance
A 5K, 10K, or more

Take a chance
believe in yourself

Take a chance
go fast!
Take a chance
Go! GO! GO!

My Light

Early morning runs

Peaceful, calm, energizing

What a gift to start the day

Thank you, Lord, for the way

You position the stars just right

To guide me as I run through the night

I know you are with me

Cheering me on

Morning or night

Running is my light

———◆———

Running Moon

Hello Moon
Good morning to you
Hanging high in the big dark sky
The clouds have made way
For your silver shine

What a joy this morning
It makes it easier to see
It's my giant light bulb
It's just as special as the sun
Following me as I run

Up and down hills, around turns too
No matter where the road travels
Or my speed
The moon is in the lead
Thank you for guiding my way
Thank you for your bright light
You make running in the dark just right

Morning Runs

Running in the morning is quiet
A peace and stillness I crave
I could run later I'm certain
Yet the morning is my favorite

Nothing but nature and my feet hitting the pavement
My breathing relaxed and steady
Pumping my arms I feel alive and ready

I'm grateful for my body and the miles I get to run
The darkness is calming
Yet at times my eyes will come undone

Is that a person up the road?
Oh no, it's just a mailbox
Is that an enormous dog coming my way
Oh the tricks my eyes play
Oops, it's a gigantic rock
Oh my!
How my imagination can fly

I giggle now as I run

Silly Julie

This is the fun

A Choice

It's a choice to run
Like most things in life
I get a choice
How nice

To get out the door
It's a practice I love
It fits like a glove

Bread and butter
Eggs with toast
Running and me
I can't disagree

We go together
Regardless of the time or medal
Nothing could be better

———◆———

The Flow

Running

It's time for me

Mind and body in sync

Nature all around me, I'm free

Flowing

Showing Up

I keep showing up
Not for anyone else but me
It's my responsibility

Lace-up my sneakers
Get out on the road
Even in the snow or rain
Sometimes it's hard to explain

It's not always easy
But I open the door
Once I start running
I know why I want more

Clear my mind
Think on thoughts that I find
True, helpful, and kind

Thoughts matter and will affect my pace
I choose the ones that will keep me in the race
Body and mind are connected all the time
Thank goodness I'll need them on this climb.

I will not whine, I'll keep showing up
Bring a good attitude
As I get to run, with gratitude

———◆———

Here I Come

Boston Marathon here I come

Many years to achieve this one

I Will keep on training

My mind is gaining

I'm running the roads as I hum

———◆———

Mindful Runs

The sentences fill my head
As my legs move and my arms swing
The training is there
The training is easy I think
It's the mind that can spiral

I need to be the watcher
Not let my thoughts drift away
To the dark side
Catch them quick
Before they make me sick

That's when I start to feel it in my body
But it starts all in my mind

I'll feel it in my stomach, my hip, and my back
My knee even wants to quack
This pain is real, no matter what
Yet it's not going to be the master
I will look after
My thoughts and what I say
I will master my mind

I will be okay

I know this discomfort
This is how it shows up
It won't knock me down
If it does, I'll get back up

———◆———

Connection

I connect to the road
So much space
Me and the great big sky
Nothing can replace

The feeling of openness
It has no end
I can run forever
Better with a friend
The sights and sounds
My breathing fills the air
I keep running without a care

The trees are all around
I connect to the ground
To the birds, to the leaves
This is the best part of running for me

To climb the hills, to fly down the other end
I feel like a kid again
This is my gift
I whisper thank you

I will not take it for granted

What a view

———◆———

The Gift

I am a runner
It's simple to do
Lace-up my sneakers
And check out the view
My body and mind working together
Nothing feels better

The wind at my back
Or the sunshine on my face
The sights and the sounds
I do appreciate
Swinging my arms
Pumping my legs

The road is my happy place

It's a gift that I love
The feeling it brings
I am alive and free
This is me!

Stars

Stars are shining bright
Staring at the great big sky
I could stay in bed
Glad I love to run instead
Outside time to clear my head

◆

A Runner

Duck behind a bush or a tree
If you're a runner
It's the way to go p, tee-he
Pop a squat
Shimmy shake
Now back to the road
You must not be late

Oh, Wait!

You have nowhere to be
Just run, stay present
Leave all your worries behind
The longer on the road
The easier you'll find
So take your time

———◆———

Moon Run

I run with the moon
And hum a tune

It's peaceful and quiet
Just me and the moon
Did I just see a raccoon

EEK!

Critters are out and about
So I keep an eye out
I never know what I will see
The moon and me

The moon and I will run
Until the miles are done
Thank you moon
See you soon

◆

Ode to Fartlek

The training run is a fartlek, to work on some speed

It keeps my mind engaged as I imagine taking the lead

Pumping my arms and relaxing my face

This will get me ready for the race

My legs moving quick and steady

I know I'm ready

My legs are strong, I was made to run

To race again and have fun

Sky Runs

I look up at the sky
It goes for miles
Wide-open as I run

I love the stars in the early morn
The moon gigantic
Their light helps shine my way
It's my guide
Until the sunrise, it's a new day

The longer I run the more I see
That the sky and everything around
Are all connected to me

Why Do I Run?

Why do I run?
It's no mystery
It's great for my health history

My heart pumping blood
My lungs are working better
I get up in the morning like a go-getter

My nerves getting a wiggle
Thinking about that makes me giggle
Even my brain changes too
It's true!

My bones getting thicker
Muscles getting stronger
No wonder why I want to run longer.

Some say I'm crazy
I know the truth
This is why I run
How about you?

Long Run

The long runs I love
The chance to see what I'm made of
I expect it will hurt
I know I will get tired
Yet what I say will keep me inspired

My brain will tell me to stop
My body will want to slow down
It's all heart at this moment
No need to back down
I'm training for a marathon
The miles stay the same
It's the mind that changes
Every step of the way

This is running
The long runs are my practice
To try on thoughts to pull me through
I can do it, and so can you!

◆

Running in Fall

Running in the Fall
Is the best season of all
The leaves are changing color
Orange, yellow, red
I keep my eyes ahead

To the beautiful views
As I climb in altitude
The air is cooler
The leaves are falling down
Careful not to step on wholly bear
As she inches across the ground

Running in Autumn
Abundant and bright
What a beautiful site
I'm grateful for the change
And find I'm more appreciative as I age
For the miles, I get to coast
And connecting with nature
That is what I love most

◆

Soaring

Some say running is boring

Could be

For me, it's captivating

Head held high

Checking out the clouds, birds, and trees

Feet flapping with the breeze

Arms pumping ready to fly

Confidence rising

Choosing thoughts that are thriving

I can do this

I am strong

A good attitude out on the road

Is the endurance runners code

Be present with what's around

So much to see and explore

Definitely not boring

Running is soaring

◆

Run Brave

Boston marathon ready
Elevation gaining and steady

It's an achievable task
My mind and body I ask
Mental strength has been the focus
Mindset is what matters most, I notice

Stay brave and calm
You got this mom!
The marathon is made for you
And this I know is true
Run Brave

I Get to Run

In five days
I get to run
The Boston Marathon

The journey has been long
I've learned self-acceptance and love
In the miles that I've run

I will join the women before me
Who gave me this opportunity
To toe the start line
Has been my dream
I made it thank you team
I will race in the moment
Run, breathe, relax
I will be grateful for this circumstance

I know the race will hurt
I will keep my mind alert
I've been practicing mantras in advance
To keep me calm and steady
My inner critic doesn't stand a chance

I can handle this
I have what it takes
I will endure...
Onward!

Can't Stop Me

The Boston Marathon is not my foe

I've been training for years though

To run heartbreak hill

Gonna be such a thrill

The pain couldn't stop me yo!

◆

Willow Tree

I saw a beautiful graceful willow tree
Hanging down inviting me
To jump up and give it a high five
You made it to Boston
Your dream of running has come alive

I couldn't be happier
A smile across my face
Feeling connected with every runner
With each stride I make
The camaraderie is intensifying
The count down to the marathon begins

Just like the willow tree
Standing tall, marvelous, and strong
We are together and unified
We are Boston Strong

The Race

The night before a race
Layout the gear
Shirt, shorts, sneakers
Hat, socks, gels
Don't forget the BIB number
And a smile
You've made it here
Through all the miles
The 8 p.m. bedtimes and
4:30 a.m. early runs
All-weather, rain, sun, wind
You showed up

Go to bed with appreciation
Reflect on all the training you have done
Gratitude for tomorrows race
No matter the outcome
Crossing the finish line is a feeling
You can't replace

Heartbreak Hill

They call it heartbreak hill
And now I know why
It's perfectly placed in the marathon
To make you dig deep
It may even make you weep

The yells and shouts from the crowd
Keeps you going and feeling proud
Your legs want to slow down but your mind says NO!
Let's go, don't stop
You're almost to the top
Don't back down
Pump your arms, shorten your stride
Lean forward and enjoy the ride

It will be hard
It will be tough
You're running in Boston
This is what you signed up for
Your dream coming true
As you take in the view
You feel a pull

It's your heart Not breaking But full

Glowing

Finishing the Boston Marathon

You will glow

Light will shine from your head

And the tips of your toes

Your smile is contagious and passersby want to know

How did the race go?

How did you do?

It's a great day to celebrate and everyone

Congratulates you!

Is it the unicorn?

The medal around your neck?

Could be

Or is it more the tradition, the history,

Boston Strong and the comeback

That connects us

The passion over fear

That brings us together

The light is spreading through the city

Connections being made

And sparks flying all around

We are glowing

Glowing

Marathoner

You made it
You crossed the finish line
As much as you hurt
The fatigue, pain, and ache
Something inside you whispers
You'll do this again

It's hard to explain
The reason why
Is it the achievement, the medal around your neck
The feelings of pride, joy, or freedom
That keeps you coming back?

It's the love of the marathon
When you run one you know
It will make you sign up again
It's addicting, I know

You're a marathoner
You love to run
Keep going, keep moving
I say this addiction is fun!

It's a gift

GO, Marathoner, GO!

About the Author

Julie B Hughes is a licensed physical therapist and marathoner. She is proud to call herself a Boston Marathon finisher! A dream come true that took many years to achieve.

She is grateful for the miles her body continues to let her run and the joy it brings her. This is her first book of poetry and is in love with writing alongside her running. Julie lives in Manlius, NY with her husband and children. She would love to connect with you at the links below.

You can connect with me on:

◔ http://hughesjulie413.wixsite.com/website

Facebook:

✉ https://www.facebook.com/juliebhughes/

Made in the USA
Middletown, DE
24 November 2021

52621153R00028